Decorative Outdoor Crafts

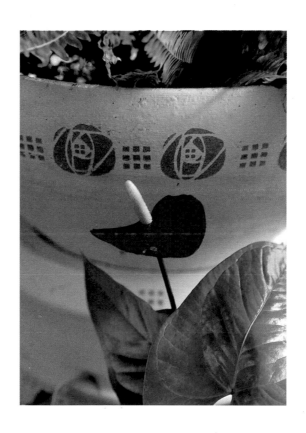

Decorative Outdoor Crafts

transforming furniture, ornaments and pots

HELEN LEVIEN

SEARCH PRESS

First published in Great Britain 2004

Search Press Limited
Wellwood, North Farm Road,
Tunbridge Wells, Kent TN2 3DR

Originally published as *Change That Garden* in 2000

ISBN 1 84448 035 6

Suppliers

If you have difficulty in obtaining any of the materials and
equipment mentioned in this book, then please visit the
Search Press website for details of suppliers:
www.searchpress.com

Alternatively, you can write to the Publishers at the address
above, for a current list of stockists, which includes firms who
operate a mail-order service.

Publisher's note
All the step-by-step photographs in this book feature
the author, Helen Levien, demonstrating how to
transform garden furniture, ornaments and pots. No
models have been used.

Colour separation by Graphics '91 Pte Ltd, Singapore
Printed by SNP SPrint (M) Sdn Bhd, Malaysia.

I would like to thank all of the following, who generously provided materials and equipment featured in this book:

A.B. Woodworking	Shaker boxes
Arty's	silk
Black & Decker	power tools and workmate
Centurion	Mackintosh stencil
Design Objectives	ceramic tiles, furniture blanks, adhesive
Edding	marker pens, cutting mats and craft knives
Evo-stik	adhesives and putty
Janomé	sewing machine, thread, scissors
John Lewis	fabric
Liquitex	acrylic paints, varnishes and mediums
3M	stencil mount
Mecnov Products Ltd	sundials
Oakthrift PLC	pullsaw and utility knife
Pro Arte	artist's brushes
Ray Munn	paints, varnishes and tools
Red Bank	chimney pots
Royal Sovereign	glass tiles and tile nippers
Sainsbury's Homebase	garden furniture, pots, stones and water pump
Scumble Goosie	blanket boxes and trug
Staedtler	silver leaf and gold size
Wilkinson Freed	wood veneer
Willowstone	birdbath

My thanks also to Chantal at Search Press for her generous support and excellent advice.

The publishers would like to thank Mr and Mrs James A Sellick of Pashley Manor Gardens, Ticehurst, Nr. Wadhurst, East Sussex TN5 7HE for providing many of the locations featured in this book. The gardens are open from April to October. Please telephone 01580 200888 for further information.

With thanks also to Country Gardens, Eridge Road, Tunbridge Wells, Kent, TN4 8HP for supplying many of the plants that appear in this book.

contents

introduction

My main aim in writing this book has been to share my design ideas with anyone who has an interest in transforming or brightening up an exterior space.

It is not necessary to own acres of landscaped garden, in fact you do not need a garden at all since most of these projects will work just as well on a patio, a doorstep, a windowsill or even in a conservatory.

Although the level of skill required varies from project to project there is nothing in this book that is difficult to achieve. The step-by-step approach, combined with clear photography and a full list of required materials, makes all the processes simple and straightforward.

My choice of colours and motifs has naturally been a personal one, so if your taste is for a different colour or design then go for it. Feel free to experiment with, adapt and improve on my ideas and above all, do not be afraid to make mistakes. They can often lead to the most rewarding discoveries.

Enjoy the process as much as the end result and your own personal style will shine through, giving each project an individual twist. Treat this book as a starting point and, wherever it takes you, enjoy the journey.

materials & equipment

This is a glossary of materials and equipment you may find helpful when using this book, or as a reference when planning other DIY projects.

Always read the safety instructions on all products and ensure proper safety precautions are observed.

TOOLS AND EQUIPMENT

electric sander	there are many electric sanding tools on the market today. A good multi-sander will cater for a wide range of tasks.
sandpaper and sanding pads	available in a wide range of grades although the most common types are simply labelled coarse, medium and fine. When sanding, it is important to move gradually from coarse to fine sandpaper to ensure a smooth finish.
wood chisel	a hand tool with a square bevelled blade for shaping wood.
planer file	a cross between a plane and a file, with a serrated blade for shaping wooden surfaces.
work bench	a stable, adjustable surface for supporting work when sawing, sanding and cutting.
G-clamp	used to hold wood in position on a work bench, or to clamp surfaces together while an adhesive is setting.
lino-cutter or burin	for cutting lino board to make prints. Kits come complete with a wooden handle and a selection of blades. They can be purchased at good art shops. When the blades become blunt they can be bought singly, which is a cheaper option than purchasing another kit.
hairdryer	used to warm and soften lino board to ease engraving. Alternatively, warm the lino on a radiator. Lino should cut like hard cheese; if it crumbles it is not warm enough.

cutting mat or art mat	should be made from a dense material that allows repeated cutting on its surface.
craft knife or scalpel	a sharp blade for precision cutting.
metal rule	it is always advisable to use a metal rule when cutting straight lines with a craft knife or scalpel, as blades are extremely sharp and will slice easily through a plastic or wooden rule.
paint kettle	a plastic or metal bucket into which a small amount of paint can be decanted from the tin, keeping the remainder clean and protected from the air.
palette	a surface on which to mix colours. You can use a scrap of wood, an old plate or an old tile for example.
palette knife	normally used for oil painting but works well as a small trowel or spreader.
tile nippers or nibblers	for cutting mosaic tiles.
grout spreader	a plastic tool with teeth, used for spreading grout.
water mister	commonly used to spray plants. It provides a thick mist of water for moistening wood-veneer.

BRUSHES, ROLLERS AND SPONGES

decorator's brushes	can be used to apply acrylics, emulsions and gloss paints. They are available in a variety of sizes. Prices vary according to the quality of bristle.
artist's brushes	standard artist's brushes come in lots of different shapes, but the most common are round and flat. Round brushes have a fine point and are excellent for detailed work, while flat brushes have a square end and (much like an italic pen nib) will produce both wide and thin strokes. Both types come in a variety of sizes. Their quality depends on the hair used, for example, sable, squirrel or hog hair. Synthetic brushes are also available.
softening brushes	a soft-bristled brush designed to blend or soften a paint effect.
stencil brushes	designed to achieve a fine covering of paint when working over a stencil. The bristles are coarse and robust which prevents paint being forced under the stencil. They are available in many sizes.
toothbrushes	can be used to spatter paint over a surface.
paint rollers and trays	give a smooth and even application of paint to a surface. Different types of rollers are available for different paints.
sponges	can be used to apply paint. Different sponges give different effects. Natural marine sponges are expensive but give a fabulous random texture to a design. Synthetic sponges are more regular and the designs created with them will reflect this – however, they can be torn into more ragged shapes and used to produce some interesting finishes.

PAINTS, VARNISHES, MEDIUMS AND MATERIALS

acrylic paint
water-soluble, non-toxic and totally weatherproof paint. It dries quickly and is available in a good range of colours. There are two types: jar colour and tube colour.

jar colour acrylics concentrated acrylic paints with a creamy consistency. They can be thinned easily with water or blended with mediums which make them ideal for applications such as airbrushing, fabric painting, watercolour techniques, mural painting, silk-screening, printmaking and illustration. They are also permanent on surfaces such as wood, stone and terracotta, and they are machine-washable on fabric. Jar colour acrylics do not show brushmarks and they contain a higher pigment load than tube colours thinned to the same consistency. This allows an excellent colour coverage with a very smooth finish.

tube colour acrylics these are of a thick buttery consistency and are designed to show textures such as brush strokes and knife marks in the manner of an oil paint. This makes them excellent for impasto (textured) techniques.

hammered-finish enamel paint
enamel paint designed for use on metal surfaces. It is available in a range of colours and dries very quickly to form a tough shell. Two or more coats are generally required for a solid finish.

emulsion paint
water-based paint which can be diluted with water or glazes, or textured with mediums. It dries in 1–3 hours. Seal with an acrylic varnish for exterior use.

acrylic varnish
a tough, water-based varnish which dries quickly to a clear finish. It is easy to work with, does not yellow and can be used over all water-based paints. It is available in matt, satin or gloss finish.

spray varnish
a varnish which works well over water-based paints. Do not use over oil-based paints as the varnish contains cellulose thinners which will act as a paint stripper. Spray varnishing is expensive and time-consuming, but it does enable you to achieve an even finish completely free of brushmarks. Always wear a mask when working with this product.

marine oil or sealant
used to preserve wood. It comes in liquid form, and soaks into the wood so that, rather than forming a protective coat like varnish, it hardens the grain.

patina
a paint pigment suspended in a clear glaze which can be used to give an aged or antique finish to a surface.

primer
a basecoat that prepares a surface ready for further applications of paint.

ceramic stucco
a textured medium used to produce impasto effects. It can be applied with a brush or palette knife. When dry it has the texture of rough plaster.

grout
a thin fluid mortar for filling gaps in tiling.

tile cleaner
a solution of hydrochloric acid used in the mosaic technique to eat away 'clouding' left behind by grout and cement. Once you have cleaned a mosaic, wash away all traces of tile cleaner or the acid will continue to erode the grout and cement.

furniture wax or beeswax	a colourless, versatile wax for polishing paintwork or furniture. It is also available coloured, for use as an antiquing or liming wax.
gold size	an adhesive base to which silver and gold is applied. It is available as water-based or oil-based. I recommend using a water-based gold size for exteriors. Seal the leaf with an acrylic varnish.
silver leaf	fine sheets of silver commonly used in picture framing. The sheets are often supplied in transfer form attached to a thin backing of tissue paper. This is particularly useful for ease of application to a sized surface. Also available in gold and bronze.
PVA adhesive (Polyvinyl Acetate)	this can be used as a primer or sealant, but it is most commonly used as an adhesive. It is quick-drying, cheap and widely available.
wood adhesive	for bonding wood. Use a weatherproof wood adhesive for exterior projects.
stencil mount adhesive	a spray adhesive which allows you to remove and reposition a stencil many times.
epoxy resin adhesive	a two-part adhesive prepared by mixing equal quantities of resin and hardener. This adhesive is quick-setting and once bonded is heat-resistant and waterproof.
wood epoxy putty	a multi-use epoxy that hardens in ten minutes. It is weatherproof and can be sanded, painted and varnished.
brown paper tape	a gum-backed paper tape, useful for holding delicate surfaces together while adhesive dries, e.g. wood veneer. Gently remove the tape by dissolving with water.
masking tape	ideal for securing designs in position as well as masking off areas. Paint has a tendency to bleed underneath masking tape so if a crisp line is desired use a clear adhesive tape instead.
carbon and tracing paper	used for transferring a design.
acetate	plastic sheet from which you can cut your own stencils.
lino board	a linoleum block which consists of a canvas backing thickly coated with a preparation of linseed oil and powdered cork. Lino board can be easily sculpted with special cutting blades to form a lino-cut for printing.
netting	use a close-weave fibre netting for mosaicing. This enables you to work on a design before attaching it to your chosen surface.
wood veneer	a thin covering of fine wood which can be applied to a coarser wood.

SAFETY AND PROTECTION

goggles	should be worn whenever there is a danger of toxic paint, mediums or varnish splashing into the eyes. You should also wear goggles when cutting mosaic tiles.
dust mask	should be worn when sanding, handling powders, or using products that give off harmful fumes. Also recommended when working with Medium Density Fibreboard.
protective gloves	essential when working with toxic substances that can cause burns or skin irritation.

rustic table

SANDING

This project came out of my desire to create a suitable piece for an untamed corner of a garden. The wood, from an oak tree brought down in the storms of 1987, has been sanded and oiled, but otherwise treated as little as possible. Any type of wood can be used. Rough timber such as a scaffolding plank or an old railway sleeper, will often have a rich and beautiful grain hidden beneath its dull, weathered exterior.

To achieve the best results you should use a succession of coarse, medium and fine sandpapers to refine the surface gradually. A coarse grade creates a new surface or shape, a medium grade smooths the new surface and the finest grade prepares it for polishing. The aim is to reveal the raw, natural beauty of the wood and to create a simple piece that is a delight both to look at and to touch.

The finished rustic table.

YOU WILL NEED

Two lengths of tree trunk and one rough-cut plank of wood

Work bench

Chisel

Hammer

Handsaw

Planer file

Electric sander

Coarse, medium and fine grade sanding pads

Cloths

Oil-based marine sealant

Protective goggles

Protective gloves

Dust mask

the project

1 Clamp the timber securely then chisel off the bark from all pieces of wood. Hold the blade with the flat surface uppermost, and gently tap with a hammer.

2 Turn the chisel the other way round and repeat the process to remove any stubborn pieces of bark.

3 To remove any protruding knots or small branch ends place a handsaw on the wood, draw it back two or three times to give a small groove, then gently let the saw cut its way through the wood. Use your index finger to steady the saw and keep it balanced as you work.

4 Use a planer file to remove rough edges and large imperfections in the wood.

5 Work over all surfaces of the wood using an electric sander fitted with a coarse sander pad.

6 Repeat step 5 with medium sandpaper, then with fine.

7 Wipe over all surfaces of the wood with a damp cloth to remove dust and debris. Leave to dry.

8 Use a cloth to flood all surfaces of the wood with oil-based marine sealant. Re-apply, then wipe clean. The tabletop shown here was heavy so I chose not to attach it to the legs. However, if you want to do so, use weatherproof wood adhesive or an epoxy adhesive.

The finished rustic table.

Railway sleepers can be secured on to sections of old telegraph poles to create low plant stands.

A variation of the rustic table.

aztec plant stand

TEXTURED STENCILLING & DRY BRUSHING

The astonishing stone carvings of Aztec mythology combined with the vibrant colours associated with Aztec art and ornamentation were my inspirations for this project. I have used textured stencilling to give a raised three-dimensional feel to the designs, and I have dry-brushed the bricks with a dusting of white paint to create a weather-worn look and to give the impression of bright colours faded over time.

Wood, stone or ordinary builder's bricks can be used for this project. The advantage of working with bricks is that they can easily be reassembled into different formations for different purposes, perhaps set into a path or as the border for a flower bed.

Aztec *characteristic of the art and culture of the Aztecs, an ancient Mexican Indian civilisation.*

The finished Aztec plant stand.

YOU WILL NEED

Ordinary builder's bricks

Acrylic paint: white and a selection of colours

Paint kettle

Decorator's brushes

Palette knife or sponge

Stencil acetate or stencil card

Stencil mount adhesive

Ceramic stucco

Masking tape

Permanent marker pen

Craft knife or scalpel

Cutting mat

Cloth

Dust mask

the project

1 Use masking tape to secure a piece of stencil acetate or stencil card over one of the Aztec designs shown on pages 94–95. Trace around the design using a permanent marker pen.

2 Place the design on a cutting mat and cut it out using a craft knife or scalpel.

3 Cover your work surface. Apply stencil mount adhesive to the back of the stencil.

Note Always wear a dust mask when working with stencil mount spray adhesive.

4 Press the stencil into position on the surface of the brick.

5 Use a palette knife or sponge to apply ceramic stucco over the stencil design.

6 Remove the stencil immediately, while the stucco is still wet. Leave to dry for approximately two hours. Wipe the stucco off the stencil with a cloth.

7 Mix up a wash of coloured acrylic paint. Use a decorator's brush to paint the whole brick. Leave to dry, then apply another coat if necessary. Leave to dry. Repeat steps 1–7 with other colours and designs until all the bricks are painted.

8 Dip a dry decorator's brush into white acrylic paint. Dab off excess colour on to a cloth then lightly dust over the brick to highlight the textured design and soften the overall colour. Leave to dry.

9 Seal the surface with a matt acrylic varnish.

Dry brushing gives a dusty, sun-baked look to the bricks, and also highlights the textured designs.

The finished Aztec plant stand.

Individual Aztec bricks set into a garden path.

roman paving stone

TRANSFER MOSAICING

Roman mosaics were often used to decorate the floors of villas or temples and as a result have generally come down to us broken and worn, with large areas of the original designs missing. However, this partial survival only seems to increase the beauty of the mosaic, reminding us how precarious its existence has been over the past two millennia. My aim in this project has been to recreate this effect.

The mosaic tiles are attached to some netting and then the netting is cemented to the paving stone. This technique of transfer mosaicing gives you the advantage of creating your design before it is permanently fixed in place. Moreover, the flexibility of the netting will allow you to mosaic a curved surface, such as a pot or a vase.

Roman *of Ancient Rome or its territory or people.*

mosaic *a picture or pattern produced by an arrangement of small, variously coloured pieces of glass or stone.*

The finished Roman paving stone and two vases worked using the same technique.

YOU WILL NEED

Paving slabs

Mosaic tiles

Ready-mix grout

Quick-mix cement

Tile cleaner

PVA adhesive

Tile nippers

Hammer

Artist's paintbrush

Paint kettle

Off-cut of wood

Scissors

Permanent pen

Trowel or palette knife

White paper

Clear plastic or greaseproof
paper

Close-weave fibre netting

Cloths

Protective goggles

Protective gloves

the project

1 Draw your design to size on a piece of white paper. Cover with netting and draw over the design with a permanent marker pen.

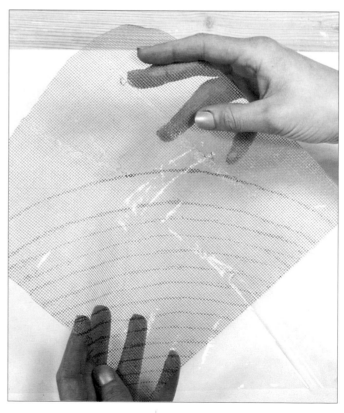

2 Remove the paper from underneath the net and replace with clear plastic or greaseproof paper. This will prevent the tiles from sticking to your work surface.

3 Use tile nippers to cut some of the tiles in half. To do this, introduce the tile about 3mm (⅛in) on to the cutting edge of the nippers. Make sure that the top of the nipper lies parallel to the top of the tile. Gently squeeze the nippers.

4 Take some of the half tiles, and repeat the process to create quarter tiles.

Note It is essential that you wear protective goggles when cutting tiles.

5 Stick the tiles into position on the netting using PVA adhesive and an artist's paintbrush. Leave to dry for approximately two hours.

6 Trim off the excess netting from around the design.

7 Place the design on to the paving slab and draw around it with a permanent pen. This will give you a guide line for where to apply the cement.

8 Mix approximately two cupfuls of cement with water, following the manufacturer's instructions. Add the water gradually so as not to make the consistency too wet. Stir thoroughly.

Note You should wear a dust mask when mixing cement.

9 Use a palette knife or small trowel to apply the cement to the paving slab within the marked design area.

11 Cover the mosaic with a board and tamp down firmly with a hammer to force the cement up through the netting. Remove the board.

10 Place the mosaic net-side down over the cemented area. Press down with your fingers.

12 Cover any edges of netting with cement.

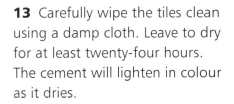

13 Carefully wipe the tiles clean using a damp cloth. Leave to dry for at least twenty-four hours. The cement will lighten in colour as it dries.

14 Apply grout between the tiles with your fingers – make sure you wear protective gloves when you do this. Wipe off excess with a damp cloth. Leave to dry for twenty-four hours.

15 Buff with tile cleaner and a damp cloth. Rinse the tile cleaner off using a very wet cloth.

Note Tile cleaner is an acid solution. It must be rinsed off or it will continue to eat into the grout and cement.

A Roman mosaic path.

Try using the technique shown in the project on pots and vases. As the design is on flexible netting, it is easy to apply to a curved surface.

You can adapt this technique to make whole designs. This more complex design was inspired by a sixth-century mosaic of St Paul in Ravenna, Italy.

victorian pot

Victorian of or characteristic of the time of Queen Victoria (1837–1901).

CREATING A SANDSTONE & LICHEN EFFECT

My inspiration for the effect used in this project came from an overgrown Victorian garden in which plant pots, ornaments and statues were being swallowed up by undergrowth, and their sandstone surfaces had been weathered by the elements and become encrusted with lichen.

In this project I show you a more easily obtainable and less time-consuming way to achieve this sandstone and lichen effect. The technique can be applied to terracotta, plaster, cement or even (if you apply a basecoat of primer first) a smooth surface such as plastic. Newly bought pots, planters, ornaments and statues can be transformed to blend harmoniously into their garden surroundings.

The finished Victorian pot.

YOU WILL NEED

Acrylic paint: titanium white, chromium oxide green or olive green, yellow oxide, raw sienna, Turner's yellow

Decorator's paint brushes

Paint kettle/palette

Synthetic sponge

Natural marine sponge

Cloth

Sand

Matt or satin varnish

Toothbrush

Water

the project

1 Mix a basecoat colour of yellow oxide, Turner's yellow and titanium white acrylic to create a pale yellow (mustard) colour. Reduce it with a little water for ease of application. Paint the whole piece inside and out. Leave to dry. Apply a second coat if required.

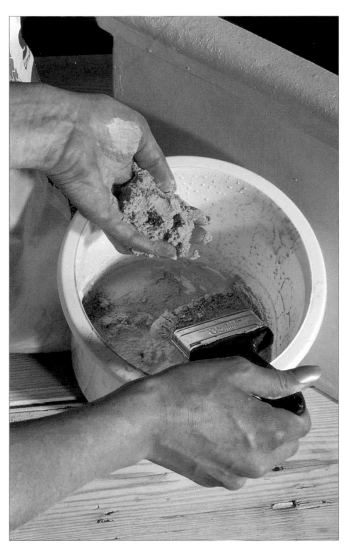

3 Brush the textured blend of sand and basecoat colour on to the pot.

2 Mix a couple of handfuls of sand with the basecoat colour.

4 Stipple over the surface with a synthetic sponge to remove brushmarks.

5 Sprinkle sand randomly over the pot to create even more texture.

6 Gently press the sand on to the surface with the sponge. Leave to dry thoroughly.

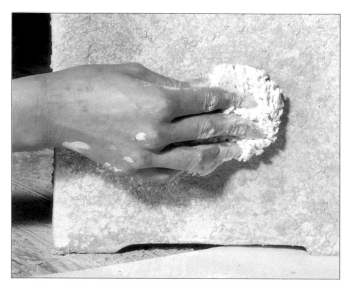

7 Dilute titanium white acrylic paint with water until it is the consistency of milk. Dip a slightly damp natural marine sponge into this white wash, then pat it on to a cloth to get rid of excess paint. Sponge on to the pot to create a patchy effect. Leave to dry.

8 Mix up a raw sienna wash (i.e. water and raw sienna) and apply randomly over the surface using a natural marine sponge (see step 7). Make sure you get into all the crevices.

9 Apply a less diluted titanium white wash to the pot, again using the natural marine sponge.

10 To simulate lichen, first mix a wash of chromium oxide green or olive green. Again, use the marine sponge to apply patches of green over the textured sand. Concentrate on the areas where the extra sand was sprinkled on.

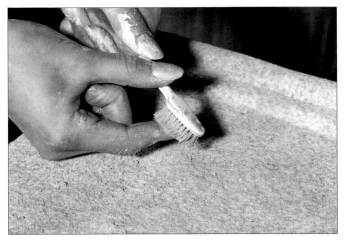

11 Mix quite a strong wash of yellow oxide and Turner's yellow. Dip a toothbrush into the wash and experiment with spattering the colour on a piece of scrap cloth.

12 Use the toothbrush to spatter the surface of the pot with yellow. Try to work over the green areas of colour only.

Note If you want to give the impression of a thicker growth of lichen you can blend the yellow and green by dabbing with a cloth.

13 When the piece is dry, apply a matt acrylic varnish to all surfaces.

Note It is important to have a very clean brush for varnishing.

Once you have applied the varnish, leave it to dry. Do not go back over it to remove brushmarks – if you do, it will create bubbles and produce a milky finish.

A terracotta pot softened by a sandstone and lichen effect.

Coarse builder's sand can be used to
create a thicker lichen effect, and to
transform an ordinary concrete birdbath.

The use of a fine-grained sand
on this plaster lion prevents the
blurring of sculptural details.

thai picnic cloth

FABRIC PRINTING

Thailand has a rich artistic tradition of painting and printing on all types of material. Beautifully decorated and intricately designed silks play a significant role both in the social and religious lives of the Thais. Animal subjects are particularly popular, often printed in a repeating pattern that runs around the perimeter of cloth.

When setting out to create my own version of a typical Thai design I chose as a motif for my fabric print one of the commonest sights on any wall or ceiling in Thailand: the gecko. I have also introduced stylised borders of undergrowth.

Thai *of or relating to Thailand or its people or language.*

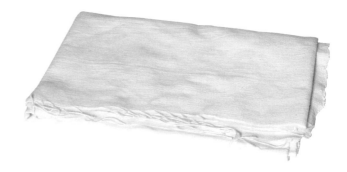

The finished Thai picnic cloth.

YOU WILL NEED

Fabric for tablecloth

Lino board

Wooden board, 12mm (½in) thick

Acrylic paint

PVA wood adhesive

Lino-cutter (burin) and small V-cutting blade and small and large U-cutting blades

Palette knife

Sponge

Tracing paper and carbon paper

Masking tape

Permanent marker pen

Pencil

Sewing machine and thread

Scissors

Newspapers/blanket

Hairdryer

the project

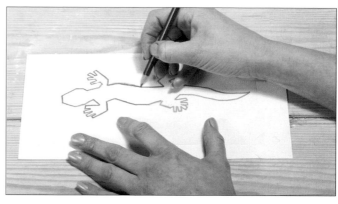

1 Place a piece of tracing paper over one of the gecko designs on page 95 and secure in place with masking tape. Trace the design using a pencil.

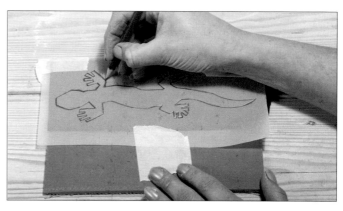

2 Place a piece of carbon paper over the lino board and put the tracing paper on top. Secure with masking tape. Transfer the gecko design by drawing around the outline with a pencil.

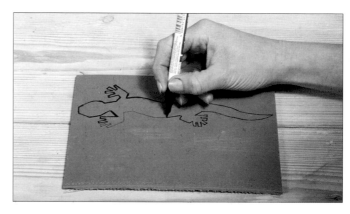

3 Remove the carbon paper. Strengthen the outline on the lino with a permanent marker pen.

4 Insert a small V-cutting blade into the lino-cutter.

5 Use a hairdryer to warm the lino. Alternatively, place the lino on a radiator or leave it in hot sunshine.

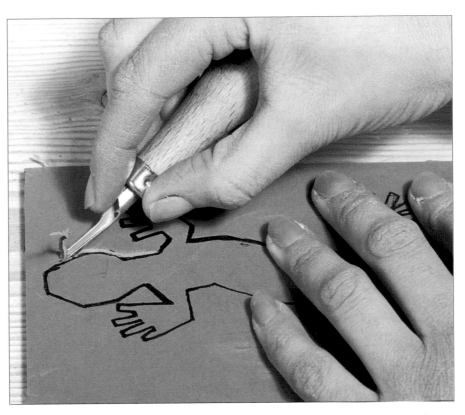

6 Push the lino-cutter around the outline of the design. Cut gently and not too deeply to start.

Note Lino should cut like a hard cheese. If it resists and crumbles, reheat it.

7 Replace the V-cutting blade with a small U-cutting blade and begin to scoop out the background. Use a large U-cutting blade to remove large areas.

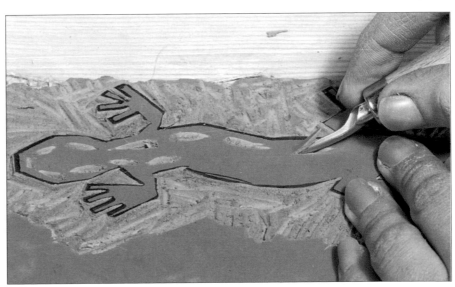

8 Use the V-cutting blade to gouge out a random pattern on the gecko's body.

9 Trim off the excess lino with scissors.

10 Use a palette knife to apply PVA wood adhesive to a piece of wooden board roughly the same size as the gecko design. Press the design on to the board, then leave to dry thoroughly.

11 Use the small and large U-cutter to make a random border design in another piece of lino. Again, glue this to a piece of wooden board.

12 Secure the edges of the fabric with an overlocking stitch. This will prevent the picnic cloth from fraying.

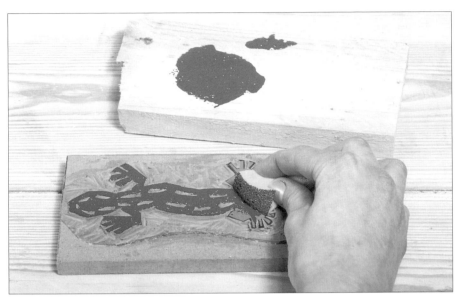

13 Sponge acrylic paint on to the raised image of one of the lino-cuts.

14 Place the fabric on a cushioned surface, e.g. a few sheets of newspaper or a blanket. Press the lino-cut on to the cloth and remove. Repeat, using both lino-cuts to build up a pattern and border. Leave to dry.

The finished Thai picnic cloth.

I have used the same gecko prints from the project to decorate deckchairs, a second picnic cloth and a gazebo. Acrylic paints are permanent and machine-washable so there is no need to heat-seal them.

shaker trug

Shaker an American
religious sect living in
rural communities.

trug a shallow
oblong garden basket
usually of wood strips.

APPLYING WOOD VENEER

Classic Shaker furnishings are always elegant, exquisitely
designed and beautifully crafted. There is a strong reliance
on plain wood, worked without fussiness or elaboration.
Many of these pieces, such as chests, oval boxes and
cupboards were made for storage (essential for maintaining
the ordered life so important to the Shakers), while trugs
were used for collecting produce or carrying tools.

To adapt a blank MDF trug into a Shaker-style piece I have
applied a quality wood veneer to its outer surfaces. The
technique of wood veneering is a relatively skilled process
and if you have not tried it before then this is a good sized
object with which to begin.

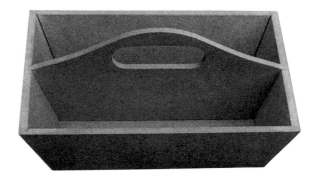

The finished Shaker trug.

YOU WILL NEED

Blank MDF trug
Wood veneer
Furniture wax
Acrylic paint
Matt acrylic varnish

Decorator's brush
Paint kettle
PVA wood adhesive
Water mister
Brown paper tape
G-clamps
Scalpel or craft knife
Flat boards
Cloths

the project

1 Use a water mister to dampen both sides of the wood veneer.

2 Press the veneer between two flat boards to prevent it from cockling. Leave for four hours.

3 Use a scalpel or craft knife to cut a piece of veneer for one of the sides of the trug. Allow at least 10mm (³⁄₈in) overlap all round for shrinkage.

Note It is best to cut veneer on a hard wooden surface, such as MDF or chipboard.

4 Use a decorator's paintbrush to apply PVA adhesive to the appropriate side of the trug. Make sure the adhesive covers the whole of this surface.

> **Note** If you are veneering a large surface, it is best to use bone adhesive (also known as pearl adhesive) rather than PVA.

5 Press the veneer on to the trug. Use a damp cloth to remove any excess adhesive.

6 Clamp into position. Allow to dry for an hour.

7 Use a scalpel to trim off the excess veneer, following the lines of the box as you work. Repeat steps 3–7 to cover the other three sides of the trug.

8 Veneer the narrow top edges in the same way as the sides, allowing approximately 3mm (⅛in) for shrinkage. However, instead of using clamps to hold the strips in position, use brown paper tape.

9 To create a neat mitred corner, use a scalpel or craft knife to cut a forty-five degree joint through both pieces of veneer.

10 Use the scalpel to remove the waste carefully from underneath the join.

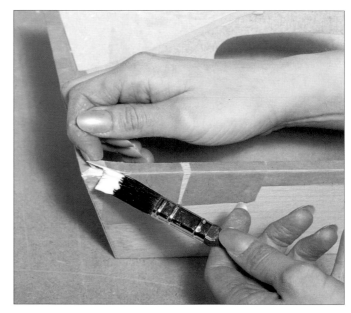

11 Apply some more adhesive under the ends of the strips. Again, use brown paper tape to secure the join – this will also prevent the veneer from shrinking back and leaving a gap. Leave to dry for an hour.

12 Moisten the brown paper tape with a damp cloth before removing it. Trim off the excess veneer.

Note If the edges of the veneer are not perfectly flush after trimming them, you can gently sand with a sanding sponge or fine grade sandpaper.

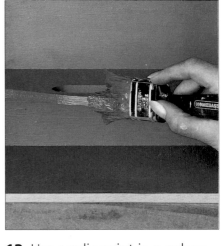

13 Use acrylic paint in a colour of your choice to paint the inside of the trug. Allow to dry.

14 Brush furniture wax on to the veneered surfaces and then buff off with a soft cloth. Repeat.

15 Apply a coat of matt acrylic varnish to the inside of the trug to seal the acrylic paint.

The finished Shaker trug.

This birch-veneered blanket chest complements perfectly the set of classic oval Shaker boxes.

This photograph shows the simplicity of the Shaker style.

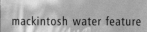

mackintosh water feature

STENCILLING ON A CURVED SURFACE

Mackintosh's pioneering and inventive style was the inspiration for this project. In particular, his lightness of touch with heavier materials and his elegant application of repeated flower motifs combined with more linear, geometric designs.

An ordinary chimney pot, with a terracotta bowl set on top, create a novel profile that reflects the strength and the delicacy of this remarkable style. The stencil is a pre-cut Mackintosh rose motif while the colours I have used to decorate this garden water feature derive from the neutral palette that he so often employed.

Charles Rennie Mackintosh 1868–1928, British architect and designer, born in Glasgow, who became a leader of the Glasgow Style, a movement related to Art Nouveau.

The finished Mackintosh water feature.

YOU WILL NEED

Chimney pot

Large terracotta bowl

Water pump and hose attachment

Cobblestones, gravel and water plants

Emulsion or acrylic paint: ivory

Acrylic paint: silver and stainless steel

Satin acrylic varnish

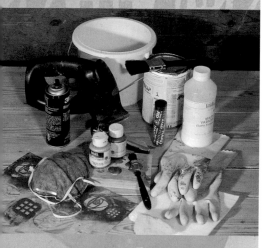

Decorator's paintbrush

Stencil brush or sponge

Electric sander – medium grade

Mackintosh rose motif stencil

Stencil mount

Epoxy putty adhesive

Scalpel or craft knife

Cloth

Protective gloves

Block of wood or palette

Paint kettle

Dust mask

the project

1 Use an electric sander with medium grade sandpaper to remove any rough edges from the chimney pot and bowl. Wear a dust mask so as not to inhale any dust.

2 Wipe over the surfaces with a damp cloth to remove any dust. Leave to dry.

3 Apply three coats of ivory emulsion or acrylic paint to the outside of the bowl and chimney pot. Allow time to dry between coats. Leave the final coat to cure for at least twenty-four hours.

4 If your terracotta bowl has a hole in the base, cut a length of epoxy putty then mix it by kneading between your fingers. Follow the manufacturer's instructions and wear protective gloves as you work.

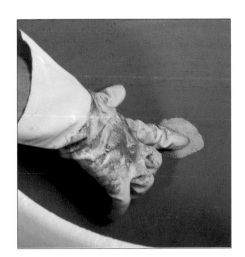

5 Use the epoxy putty to bung the hole in the base of the bowl. Allow to dry for at least an hour.

Note If you prefer, you can run the water pump lead through the hole and then putty around it.

6 Paint the inside of the bowl using silver acrylic. Leave to dry, then seal with a satin acrylic varnish.

8 Roughly mix silver with stainless steel acrylic paint. Dab a stencil brush or sponge into the paint, then pat off excess on a cloth or scrap paper.

> **Note** Do not use too much paint on the brush or sponge, or it will leak under the stencil.

7 Apply a good coverage of stencil mount adhesive to the back of the stencil. Position it on the surface of the bowl, working small sections at a time.

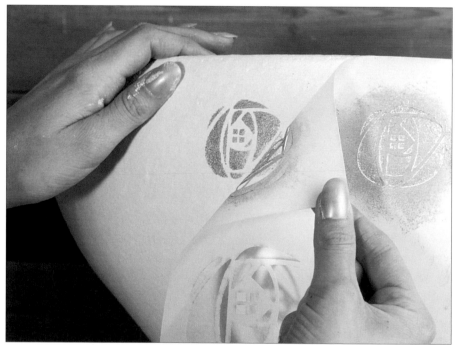

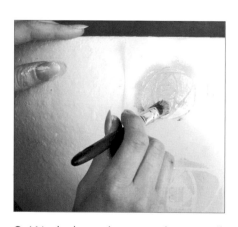

9 Work the paint over the stencil design. If you are using a brush, use a stippling motion, keeping the brush upright. If you are using a sponge, pat it gently on to the surface.

10 Remove the stencil immediately, then allow the paint to dry before going on to the next section. Repeat steps 7-9, until the bowl and chimney pot are decorated. Leave to dry.

> **Note** As you are working, it is advisable to clean the paint off the stencil regularly to maintain crisp edges.

11 Seal with a coat of satin acrylic varnish. Leave to dry for at least an hour.

12 Place a thin layer of gravel in the bottom of the bowl, then install your water pump and hose attachment on top, following the manufacturer's instructions.

13 Cover the pump and disguise the lead with cobblestones and gravel.

14 Fill the bowl with water then turn the pump on. When you can see how the water is cascading, add water plants, extra cobblestones and gravel, and any finishing touches such as a small sculpture or an arrangement of polished coins.

The finished Mackintosh water feature.

The stylised rose motif framed by a repeating geometrical pattern is a notable example of Mackintosh design.

You can adapt the project to create stunning planters. Here, I have used three different heights of chimney pot and three different sizes of bowl to create a miniature tiered garden.

japanese planet pot

raku a kind of
traditional Japanese
earthenware, usually
lead-glazed.

CREATING A FAUX RAKU EFFECT

The raku firing process is complex and its results are
unpredictable. The pot is not allowed to cool after firing but
is removed from the kiln while still glowing hot and placed in
a container filled with combustible materials such as leaves,
straw, newspaper or sawdust. These ignite, giving off smoke
and carbons. The result is a crazing and blackening of the
glaze. No two raku pots are ever the same.

I set out to recreate a raku pot using paint effects on a simple
spherical terracotta pot. Whilst I was experimenting with the
technique, I noticed a chance resemblance to the surface of the
moon. A series of 'planet' pots followed, each one
individually worked and coloured. Unless you
happen to have a kiln, and a great deal of
patience, this is probably your best bet for
creating a raku pot.

The finished Japanese planet pot, with two other colour variations.

YOU WILL NEED

Spherical pot (or similar shape)

Electric sander

Sandpaper – fine and medium grade

Acrylic paint: White and three shades of blue

Gloss or semi-gloss spray varnish

Softening brush

Synthetic and natural marine sponges

Scrap of wood or palette

Cloth

Dust mask

the project

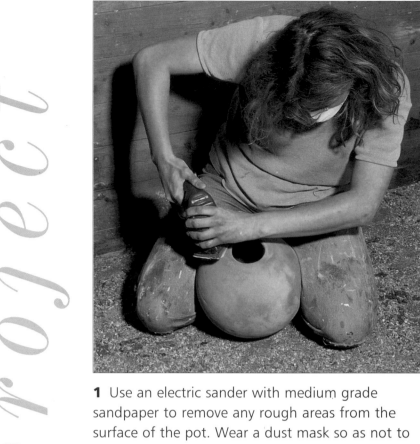

1 Use an electric sander with medium grade sandpaper to remove any rough areas from the surface of the pot. Wear a dust mask so as not to inhale any dust.

2 Wipe over the surface of the pot with a damp cloth to remove any dust. Allow to dry.

4 Use the sponge to blend the colours on the surface. Remember to sponge just inside the rim as well. Leave to dry. Repeat if necessary.

3 Pour out equal quantities of the three shades of blue acrylic paint on to a piece of wood or palette. Use a slightly damp synthetic sponge to apply the colours to the pot.

Note As a colour reference, you could use images of the planets in our solar system. For example, the deep reds of Mars, the greens and blues beneath the clouds of Earth, or the silvery-grey of the Moon.

5 Mix up a wash of white acrylic. Use a natural marine sponge to apply white cloud-like areas over the blue. Leave to dry.

6 Use a softening brush as you work, to waft gently over the white areas. Leave to dry.

7 Sponge neat white acrylic paint over areas of the pale white to add depth. Allow to dry.

8 Seal with several layers of spray varnish. Hold the spray approximately 300mm (12in) away as you work. Leave to dry.

> **Note** Spray varnish gives a very even finish. However, it is essential to wear a dust mask when using it.
>
> If you prefer to use a non-spray varnish, apply it with a sponge to avoid getting brushmarks.

9 Use fine grade sandpaper to sand the surface and remove any imperfections. Wipe off any residue with a damp cloth, then apply a second coat of varnish. Leave to dry.

Japanese planet pots can be placed amid white gravel, cobblestones and rocks to create a miniature Japanese garden. The screens were made using ordinary garden trellis backed with silk.

Planet pots can also be used as ornaments. Here they are placed in a gentle waterfall.

A single exotic plant can look stunning when planted in a planet pot.

This flower arrangement is perfect for a porch or conservatory. Placed in gravel, a spherical pot will be held securely in an upright position.

A planet pot candle holder.

catalan sundial

DIRECT MOSAICING

The inspiration for this project comes from the Barcelona mosaics of the Catalan architect and artist Antoni Gaudí (1852–1926). Gaudí was a pioneer of exterior mosaic. He would work it across the façade and roof of a building in an organic, surreal design, using an extraordinary variety of materials – from shattered ceramic tiles and bottle-glass to pieces of discarded plate and even china dolls. His application of mosaic to three-dimensional forms such as sculpture, columns, flights of steps and roof turrets was a startling innovation which is just as impressive today.

This project is a fitting homage to the remarkable imagination of Antoni Gaudí. I have transformed a chimney pot into a sundial using a direct mosaicing technique – this involves attaching shattered ceramic tiles directly to the chimney pot surface.

The finished Catalan
sundial and a variation.

YOU WILL NEED

Sundial

Chimney pot

Selection of ceramic or glass tiles

Tile nippers

Protective goggles

PVA adhesive

Ready-mixed grout

Cloths

Soapy water or tile cleaner

Acrylic paint: white

Decorator's paintbrush

Synthetic sponge

Protective gloves

Scrap cardboard or grout spreader

Paint kettle

the project

1 Mix white acrylic with a small amount of water. Paint the top and bottom sections of the chimney pot using either a brush or a sponge. Apply two to three coats for total coverage, allowing time to dry between coats.

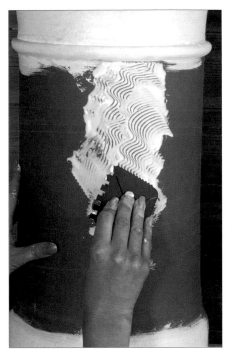

2 Use tile nippers to cut a selection of tiles into random shapes. Introduce the blades of the nippers into the tile, about 3mm (⅛in) from the edge, then gently squeeze.

Note It is essential that you wear protective goggles when cutting tiles.

3 Apply PVA adhesive to a small area of the pot. Use a grout spreader or a scrap piece of cardboard to spread it out evenly.

4 Stick the cut tiles into position over the adhesive to create your mosaic. Apply another section of adhesive, and repeat until the middle section of the chimney pot is covered. Leave to dry overnight.

5 Sponge grout over the surface of the mosaic, making sure you push it into all the crevices.

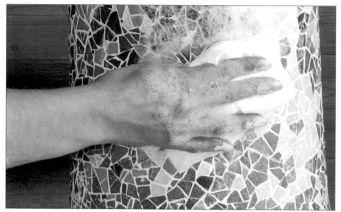

7 Rub over the surface with clean soapy water, then buff off with a clean cloth.

> **Note** For a deeper shine, or for stubborn grout, buff with tile cleaner (see page 31). Remember to wear protective gloves when you do this.

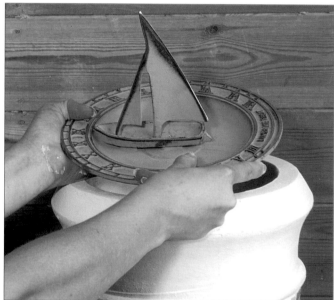

8 Set your sundial on the top of the chimney pot. Position the finished piece in your garden and then orientate it to tell the correct time.

> **Note** If your sundial is too small for the diameter of the chimney pot, cut a circle of wood, paint it white and use an epoxy resin adhesive to attach it to the chimney pot, and to secure the sundial to the wood.

6 Wipe off excess grout with a slightly damp cloth then leave for twenty-four hours.

An alternative use for the mosaiced chimney pot.

This giant lizard sculpture is inspired by Gaudí's treatment of a similar subject in the Parc Güell, Barcelona.

Mosaic on a terracotta pot.

swedish bench

Swedish *of or relating to Sweden or its people or language.*

antiquing *an applied decorative effect giving the appearance of age.*

ANTIQUING

The Swedish style is elegant and simple and will work in almost any setting. The interior designs of Carl Larsson (1853–1919) typify the Swedish style. Furniture is painted in a range of cool colours, accentuating its crisp, simple lines.

Over time, paint and varnish will deteriorate and mellow, while scratches and natural wear add character, and repeated waxing and polishing build up a rich patina. This was the effect I wanted to achieve. To replicate this, I have applied a burnt umber patina glaze to a freshly painted bench. These patinas come in a range of colours and once buffed back, highlight the grain of the wood. The finished result is a simple painted Swedish bench softened with time.

The finished Swedish bench and two chairs created using the same technique.

YOU WILL NEED

Bench

Emulsion: ivory

Primer

Patina: burnt umber

Decorator's paintbrushes

Softener brush

Paint kettle

Cloths

Matt acrylic varnish

the project

1 Prime the surface of the bench. Leave to dry.

2 Apply a coat of ivory emulsion. Leave to dry, then apply another coat. Leave overnight.

4 Stipple over the patina with a softener brush, then gently waft over the surface in different directions to soften the effect. Allow to dry for twenty-four hours.

> **Note** As you work, wipe the bristles of the softener brush on a cloth to stop them from becoming too saturated with patina.

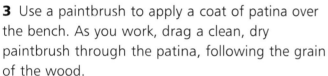

3 Use a paintbrush to apply a coat of patina over the bench. As you work, drag a clean, dry paintbrush through the patina, following the grain of the wood.

5 Use a slightly damp cloth to buff the patina and push it into the wood grain to achieve an antique look.

> **Note** Do not press too hard when you are buffing, so as not to remove all the patina. If the finished effect looks too light and you want to intensify the colour, simply repeat steps 3–5.

6 Use a new or very clean brush to apply a coat of matt acrylic varnish. Leave to dry.

The finished Swedish bench.

Changing the colour of the paint and/or patina will create interesting variations.

The Swedish style adds a cool elegance to any garden.

retro
table

Retro reviving or harking back to the fashions or styles of the 1960s.

CREATING A METALLIC FINISH

The sixties saw an explosion of new materials being employed in industry and the manufacture of consumer goods. Novel applications for metals and alloys revolutionised the construction of everything from the automobile to the soup can, and metal paints were applied to unlikely surfaces such as plastic or wood to create gleaming 'Space Age' designs.

With this project I set out to give an ordinary wooden table the Retro look, by applying a metallic finish. I have used a type of hammered-finish enamel paint which dries to give the effect of beaten metal. In addition, I have applied a design in silver leaf. The result is a hard-wearing but stylish piece of garden furniture that looks good both in sunshine and under a layer of frost.

The finished Retro table.

YOU WILL NEED

Table

Oil-based primer

Hammered-finish enamel paint: stainless steel or silver

Acrylic paint: dark blue

Decorator's brushes

Small roller and tray

Gold size

Silver leaf

Soft round brush (blusher brush)

Scissors

Acrylic varnish: satin or gloss

Protective gloves

the project

1 Prime the table top with an oil-based primer. Wear protective gloves as you work. Leave to dry.

2 Paint the legs of the table using hammered-finish enamel paint to give a beaten metal finish. Allow to dry then apply a second coat. Again, leave to dry.

> **Note** Always work in a well-ventilated room or wear a mask when using hammered-finish enamel paint.

3 Use a small roller to apply dark blue acrylic paint to the table top and around the sides. Allow to dry. Apply a second coat if necessary, and allow to dry.

Note You can use masking tape to mask off the top of the legs from the blue paint to get a crisp line.

4 Paint a wide strip of gold size on to the tabletop. Leave for approximately ten minutes, until it is tacky.

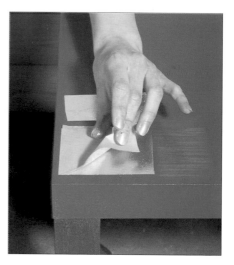

5 Cut silver leaf into squares and rectangles of various shapes and sizes. Do not remove from the backing paper.

6 Place the silver leaf squares and rectangles face down on the gold size. Gently tap over the backing paper with a soft brush to ensure that the leaf sticks to the gold size.

7 Moisten your finger, then carefully lift off the backing paper. Repeat steps 4–7 to cover the tabletop, leaving a square in the centre undecorated.

8 Use a small brush to tidy up the edges of the silver leaf with dark blue acrylic paint. Allow to dry.

9 Seal with at least five coats of acrylic varnish. Allow time to dry between coats.

Chairs can be painted using the same technique as the table. Rather than decorating the whole chair, you can concentrate on a small area. Plain ceramic vases and cobblestones can also be transformed using hammered-finish enamel paints.

patterns

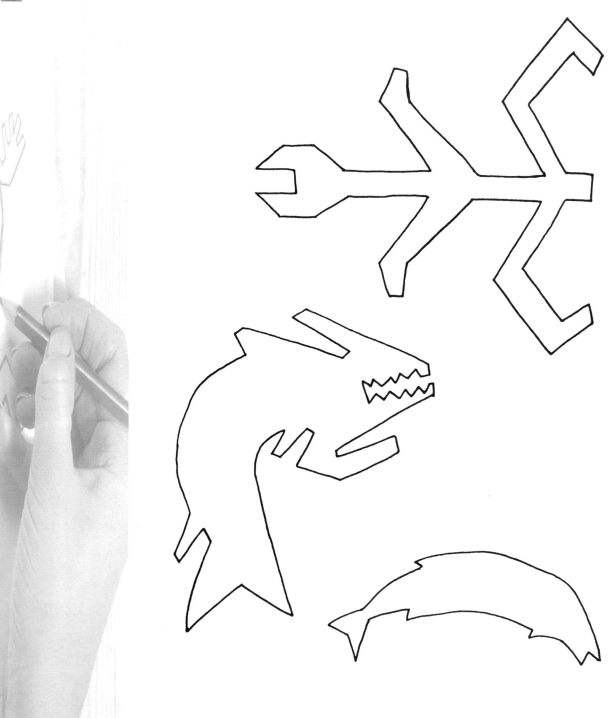

Patterns for the Aztec plant stand

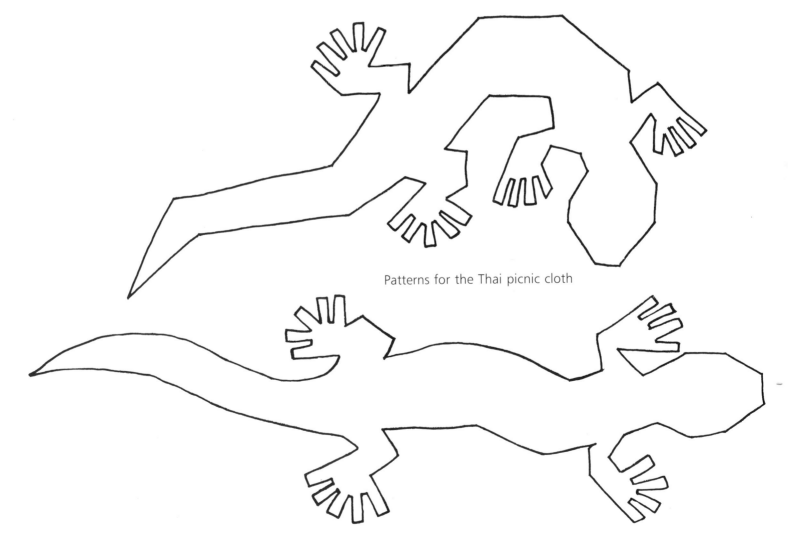

Pattern for the Aztec plant stand

Patterns for the Thai picnic cloth

index